Success With
Math Tests

D1361298

MSCHOLASTIC

Scholastic Inc. grants teachers permission to photocopy the reproducible pages from this book for classroom use.
No other part of this publication may be reproduced in whole or in part, or stored in a retrieval system,
or transmitted in any form or by any means, electronic, mechanical, photocopying,
recording, or otherwise without written permission of the publisher. For information regarding
permission, write to Scholastic Inc., 557 Broadway, New York, NY 10012.

Editor: Ourania Papacharalambous
Educational consultant: Michael Priestley
Cover design by Tannaz Fassihi; cover illustration by Kevin Zimmer
Interior design by Michelle H. Kim

ISBN 978-1-338-79846-3
Scholastic Inc., 557 Broadway, New York, NY 10012
Copyright © 2022 Scholastic Inc.
All rights reserved. Printed in the U.S.A.
First printing, January 2022

1 2 3 4 5 6 7 8 9 10   40   29 28 27 26 25 24 23 22

TABLE OF CONTENTS

INTRODUCTION

In this book, you will find eight Practice Tests designed to help students prepare to take standardized tests. Each test has multiple-choice items that closely resemble the kinds of questions students will have to answer on "real" tests. Each part of the test will take 30–40 minutes for students to complete.

The math skills measured in these tests and the types of questions are based on detailed analyses and correlations with many widely used standardized tests and curriculum standards.

How to Use the Tests

Tell students how much time they will have to complete the test. Encourage them to work quickly and carefully and to keep track of the remaining time—just as they would in a real testing session. You may have students mark their answers directly on the test pages, or you may have them use a copy of the **Answer Sheet**. A copy of the answer sheet appears at the end of each test. The answer sheet will help students become accustomed to filling in bubbles on a real test. It may also make the tests easier for you to score.

We do not recommend the use of calculators. For Practice Tests 2 and 6, students will need an inch ruler and a centimeter ruler to answer some of the questions.

At the back of this book, you will find **Tested Skills** charts and **Answer Keys** for the eight Practice Tests. The Tested Skills charts list the skills measured in each test and the test questions that measure each skill. These charts may be helpful to you in determining what kinds of questions students answered incorrectly, what skills they may be having trouble with, and who may need further instruction in particular skills. To score a Practice Test, refer to the Answer Key for that test. The Answer Key lists the correct response to each question.

To score a Practice Test, go through the test and mark each question answered correctly. Add the total number of questions answered correctly to find the student's test score. To find a percentage score, divide the number answered correctly by the total number of questions. For example, the percentage score for a student who answers 20 out of 25 questions correctly is $20 \div 25 = 0.80$, or 80%. You might want to have students correct their own tests. This will give them a chance to see where they made mistakes and what they need to do to improve their scores on the next test.

On the next page of this book, you will find **Test-Taking Tips**. You may want to share these tips and strategies with students before they begin working on the Practice Tests.

  © Scholastic Inc.

TEST-TAKING TIPS: MATHEMATICS

1 For each part of the test, read the directions carefully so you know what to do. Then, read the directions again—just to make sure.

2 Look for key words and phrases to help you decide what each question is asking and what kind of computation you need to do. Examples of key words: *less than, greatest, least, farther, longest, divided equally.*

3 To help solve a problem, write a number sentence or equation.

4 Use scrap paper (or extra space on the test page) to write down the numbers and information you need to solve a problem.

5 If a question has a picture or diagram, study it carefully. Draw your own picture or diagram if it will help you solve a problem.

6 Try to solve each problem before you look at the answer choices. (In some tests, the correct answer may not be given, so you will want to be sure of your answer. In these Practice Tests, some of the Math questions use "NG" for "Not Given.")

7 Check your work carefully before you finish. (For many questions, you can check your answer by working backwards to see if the numbers work out correctly.)

8 If you are not sure which answer is correct, cross out every answer that you know is wrong. Then make your best guess.

9 To complete a number sentence or equation, try all the answer choices until you find the one that works.

10 When working with fractions, always reduce (or rename) the fractions to their lowest parts. When working with decimals, keep the decimal points lined up correctly.

Practice Test 1: Numeration and Number Concepts

Directions. Choose the best answer to each question. Mark your answer.

1 In 1999, people in the United States held about $1,755,000 in $5,000 bills. How is 1,755,000 written in words?

Ⓐ seventeen million five hundred fifty thousand

Ⓑ one hundred thousand seven hundred fifty-five

Ⓒ one million seven hundred fifty-five thousand

Ⓓ one thousand seven hundred fifty-five

2 The country of South Africa covers an area of four hundred seventy-one thousand nine miles. How is the area written as a numeral?

Ⓐ 471,009

Ⓑ 400,071,009

Ⓒ 400,710,009

Ⓓ 470,109

3 40,000 + 500 + 6 =

Ⓐ 40,506

Ⓑ 45,600

Ⓒ 40,000,506

Ⓓ 40,500,006

4 The chart shows the area of the four largest U.S. national parks, all of them in Alaska.

National Park	Area (acres)
Denali	4,740,912
Gates of the Arctic	7,523,898
Katmai	3,674,530
Wrangell-Saint Elias	8,323,618

Which national park is largest?

Ⓐ Denali

Ⓑ Gates of the Arctic

Ⓒ Katmai

Ⓓ Wrangell-Saint Elias

5 An organization has a sign at its national headquarters showing the number of members. One of the digits has fallen from the sign.

MEMBERS
4 5   3 6 2 5

The missing digit represents what place value?

Ⓐ hundreds

Ⓑ thousands

Ⓒ ten thousands

Ⓓ hundred thousands

GO ON

© Scholastic Inc.

Practice Test 1 *(continued)*

6 The chart below lists four languages commonly spoken in U.S. homes, other than English.

Language	# of Speakers
Tagalog	1,610,000
French	1,281,300
Chinese	2,900,000
Spanish	43,200,000

Which list shows the languages from greatest to least number of speakers?

(A) French, Tagalog, Chinese, Spanish

(B) Spanish, Chinese, Tagalog, French

(C) Chinese, French, Tagalog, Spanish

(D) Spanish, Chinese, French, Tagalog

7 Lake Superior covers an area of about 31,700 square miles. What is that number rounded to the nearest ten thousand miles?

(A) 40,000

(B) 32,000

(C) 31,000

(D) 30,000

8 56, 47, 38, _____, 20, 11, 2 . . .

What number goes in the blank space in this number pattern?

(A) 30   (C) 27

(B) 29   (D) 20

9 Which of these must be an odd number?

(A) the sum of an odd number and an odd number

(B) the sum of an even number and an even number

(C) the sum of an odd number and an even number

(D) the product of an even number and an even number

10 At their annual bird count, the members of the Birders Association saw 3504 Canada geese, 1461 Brant geese, and 542 snow geese. <u>About</u> how many geese did they see in all?

(A) 5500

(B) 5000

(C) 4500

(D) 4000

11 $0 \times \frac{1}{2} (\frac{1}{4} + \frac{1}{2}) =$

(A) 0

(B) $\frac{1}{8} + \frac{1}{2}$

(C) $0 + \frac{1}{4}$

(D) $\frac{1}{8} + \frac{1}{4}$

GO ON

Practice Test 1 *(continued)*

12 Brandon has organized his music collection of 123 albums. His sister has a collection of 56 albums. <u>About</u> how much larger is Brandon's collection than his sister's?

Ⓐ twice as large

Ⓑ three times as large

Ⓒ four times as large

Ⓓ five times as large

13 What is the greatest common factor of 8, 12, and 24?

Ⓐ 2

Ⓑ 4

Ⓒ 6

Ⓓ 8

14 What is the least common multiple of 9 and 27?

Ⓐ 3

Ⓑ 27

Ⓒ 54

Ⓓ 243

15 Look at the number line.

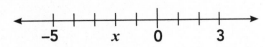

What number belongs in the place marked with an *x*?

Ⓐ −4

Ⓑ −3

Ⓒ −2

Ⓓ 2

16 Which number line shows the sum of -2 and 4?

Ⓐ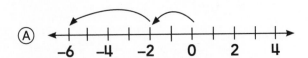

Ⓑ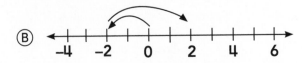

Ⓒ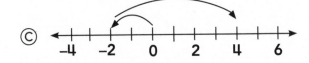

Ⓓ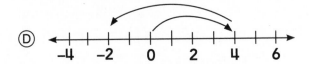

17 Alex has 8 gerbils, and 5 of them are light brown. What fraction of Alex's gerbils are light brown?

Ⓐ $\frac{3}{8}$

Ⓑ $\frac{3}{5}$

Ⓒ $\frac{5}{8}$

Ⓓ $\frac{3}{4}$

18 On Saturday, 45 of the 50 frogs' eggs in an aquarium hatched. What fraction of the frogs' eggs hatched?

Ⓐ $\frac{1}{10}$

Ⓑ $\frac{1}{5}$

Ⓒ $\frac{4}{5}$

Ⓓ $\frac{9}{10}$

GO ON ➡

© Scholastic Inc.

Practice Test 1 *(continued)*

19 Which trail through the Forbidden Swamp is longest?

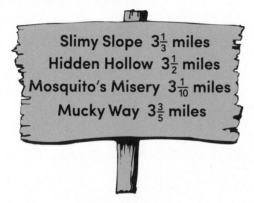

Slimy Slope $3\frac{1}{3}$ miles
Hidden Hollow $3\frac{1}{2}$ miles
Mosquito's Misery $3\frac{1}{10}$ miles
Mucky Way $3\frac{3}{5}$ miles

Ⓐ Slimy Slope
Ⓑ Hidden Hollow
Ⓒ Mosquito's Misery
Ⓓ Mucky Way

20 In which list are the fractions arranged from least to greatest?

Ⓐ $\frac{9}{10}, \frac{4}{5}, \frac{6}{8}, \frac{6}{9}$

Ⓑ $\frac{4}{5}, \frac{6}{9}, \frac{6}{8}, \frac{9}{10}$

Ⓒ $\frac{6}{9}, \frac{6}{8}, \frac{4}{5}, \frac{9}{10}$

Ⓓ $\frac{4}{5}, \frac{6}{8}, \frac{6}{9}, \frac{9}{10}$

21 In a movie theater, 75 of the 225 seats are filled. What fraction of the seats are in use?

Ⓐ $\frac{1}{5}$ Ⓒ $\frac{2}{5}$

Ⓑ $\frac{1}{3}$ Ⓓ $\frac{2}{3}$

22 Which decimal number is equal to $\frac{2}{5}$?

Ⓐ 0.10 Ⓒ 0.30
Ⓑ 0.20 Ⓓ 0.40

23 At a track-and-field meet, the top 4 runners finished the 100-meter hurdles in the following times:

18.84 seconds
18.63 seconds
18.70 seconds
18.81 seconds

Which list shows the times in order from fastest to slowest?

Ⓐ 18.63, 18.70, 18.81, 18.84
Ⓑ 18.63, 18.70, 18.84, 18.81
Ⓒ 18.70, 18.81, 18.63, 18.84
Ⓓ 18.84, 18.81, 18.70, 18.63

24 Janice found the following prices for a 96-ounce jug of apple juice. How much does the least expensive jug of juice cost?

Ⓐ $3.69 Ⓒ $3.75
Ⓑ $3.96 Ⓓ $3.84

25 Which expression is equivalent to

$4 \times (y + 9)$?

Ⓐ $(4 \times y) + 9$
Ⓑ $4 \times y \times 9$
Ⓒ $4 + y + 9$
Ⓓ $(4 \times y) + (4 \times 9)$

STOP

Answer Sheet

Student Name _____ Grade _____

Teacher Name _____ Date _____

MATHEMATICS

1 Ⓐ Ⓑ Ⓒ Ⓓ Ⓔ	**11** Ⓐ Ⓑ Ⓒ Ⓓ Ⓔ	**21** Ⓐ Ⓑ Ⓒ Ⓓ Ⓔ
2 Ⓐ Ⓑ Ⓒ Ⓓ Ⓔ	**12** Ⓐ Ⓑ Ⓒ Ⓓ Ⓔ	**22** Ⓐ Ⓑ Ⓒ Ⓓ Ⓔ
3 Ⓐ Ⓑ Ⓒ Ⓓ Ⓔ	**13** Ⓐ Ⓑ Ⓒ Ⓓ Ⓔ	**23** Ⓐ Ⓑ Ⓒ Ⓓ Ⓔ
4 Ⓐ Ⓑ Ⓒ Ⓓ Ⓔ	**14** Ⓐ Ⓑ Ⓒ Ⓓ Ⓔ	**24** Ⓐ Ⓑ Ⓒ Ⓓ Ⓔ
5 Ⓐ Ⓑ Ⓒ Ⓓ Ⓔ	**15** Ⓐ Ⓑ Ⓒ Ⓓ Ⓔ	**25** Ⓐ Ⓑ Ⓒ Ⓓ Ⓔ
6 Ⓐ Ⓑ Ⓒ Ⓓ Ⓔ	**16** Ⓐ Ⓑ Ⓒ Ⓓ Ⓔ	**26** Ⓐ Ⓑ Ⓒ Ⓓ Ⓔ
7 Ⓐ Ⓑ Ⓒ Ⓓ Ⓔ	**17** Ⓐ Ⓑ Ⓒ Ⓓ Ⓔ	**27** Ⓐ Ⓑ Ⓒ Ⓓ Ⓔ
8 Ⓐ Ⓑ Ⓒ Ⓓ Ⓔ	**18** Ⓐ Ⓑ Ⓒ Ⓓ Ⓔ	**28** Ⓐ Ⓑ Ⓒ Ⓓ Ⓔ
9 Ⓐ Ⓑ Ⓒ Ⓓ Ⓔ	**19** Ⓐ Ⓑ Ⓒ Ⓓ Ⓔ	**29** Ⓐ Ⓑ Ⓒ Ⓓ Ⓔ
10 Ⓐ Ⓑ Ⓒ Ⓓ Ⓔ	**20** Ⓐ Ⓑ Ⓒ Ⓓ Ⓔ	**30** Ⓐ Ⓑ Ⓒ Ⓓ Ⓔ

© Scholastic Inc.

Practice Test 2: Geometry and Measurement

Directions. Choose the best answer to each question. Mark your answer.

1 Which figure is a hexagon?

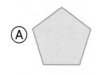 Ⓐ   Ⓒ

 Ⓑ    Ⓓ

2 Mr. Blake's driveway is 9 yards long. How many feet is that?

Ⓐ 3 ft
Ⓑ 12 ft
Ⓒ 18 ft
Ⓓ 27 ft

3 Which figure shows a line of symmetry?

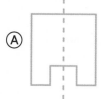 Ⓐ   Ⓒ

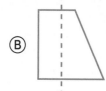 Ⓑ   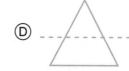 Ⓓ

4 Melanie made a diagram of her rectangular vegetable garden. What is the area of her garden?

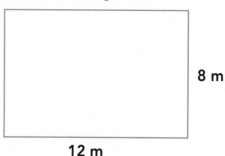

12 m / 8 m

Ⓐ 20 m²
Ⓑ 40 m²
Ⓒ 96 m²
Ⓓ 192 m²

5 This table shows the costs for overnight delivery of packages.

Overnight Delivery	
Package Weight	Rate
0 – 1.0 lb	$13.95
1.1 – 2.0 lb	$16.95
2.1 – 5.0 lb	$18.95
5.1 – 10.0 lb	$20.95
10.1 – 20.0 lb	$22.95

What is the cost for overnight delivery of a package that weighs 8.5 pounds?

Ⓐ $13.95
Ⓑ $16.95
Ⓒ $18.95
Ⓓ $20.95

GO ON

Practice Test 2 *(continued)*

6 In which pair are the triangles congruent?

Ⓐ

Ⓑ

Ⓒ

Ⓓ

7 A trapezoid is a special quadrilateral in which only one pair of opposite sides are parallel. Which figure is a trapezoid?

Ⓐ   Ⓒ

Ⓑ   Ⓓ

Use the picture to answer questions 8 and 9.

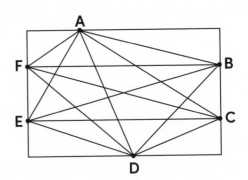

8 Which line segment is parallel to $\overleftrightarrow{FB}$?

Ⓐ $\overleftrightarrow{AD}$ Ⓒ $\overleftrightarrow{EC}$

Ⓑ $\overleftrightarrow{FD}$ Ⓓ $\overleftrightarrow{EB}$

9 Which is a right angle?

Ⓐ $\angle AFB$ Ⓒ $\angle BCD$

Ⓑ $\angle FEC$ Ⓓ $\angle DEF$

10 Which figure shows figure WXYZ after a slide?

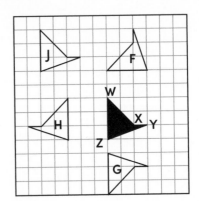

Ⓐ Figure F   Ⓒ Figure H

Ⓑ Figure G   Ⓓ Figure J

GO ON

© Scholastic Inc.

Practice Test 2 *(continued)*

11 Which white figure shows where the shaded figure would be if the graph paper were folded along the dark line?

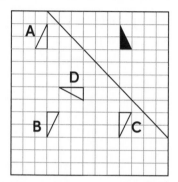

Ⓐ Figure A   Ⓒ Figure C
Ⓑ Figure B   Ⓓ Figure D

12 The rectangular yard at a dog kennel is 60 feet long and 35 feet wide. What is the perimeter of the yard?

Ⓐ 25 ft   Ⓒ 190 ft
Ⓑ 95 ft   Ⓓ 2100 ft

13 This figure is made of 1-centimeter cubes. What is the volume of the figure?

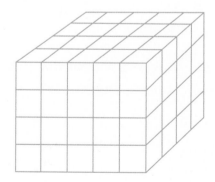

Ⓐ 20 cm^3 Ⓒ 80 cm^3
Ⓑ 56 cm^3 Ⓓ 320 cm^3

14 Jan's plane took off at 11:35 A.M. Her watch showed this time when the plane landed. How long was the flight?

Ⓐ 1 hour, 35 minutes
Ⓑ 2 hours, 25 minutes
Ⓒ 10 hours, 25 minutes
Ⓓ 10 hours, 35 minutes

15 Tim's clock stopped one afternoon at the time shown.

Later, at 6:05 P.M., he noticed that it had stopped. For how long had the clock been stopped?

Ⓐ 2 hours, 20 minutes
Ⓑ 3 hours, 45 minutes
Ⓒ 4 hours, 25 minutes
Ⓓ 8 hours, 15 minutes

16 Which unit should be used to measure the length of a driveway?

Ⓐ inches
Ⓑ gallons
Ⓒ miles
Ⓓ yards

GO ON

Practice Test 2 *(continued)*

17 What is the length of the caterpillar? (Use a centimeter ruler.)

- Ⓐ 4.6 cm
- Ⓒ 6.4 cm
- Ⓑ 6 cm
- Ⓓ 7.6 cm

18 75 centimeters is equivalent to —

- Ⓐ 0.75 m
- Ⓒ 7500 mm
- Ⓑ 7.5 m
- Ⓓ 0.075 km

19 Four men and 2 women step into an elevator. The combined weight of these adults is probably closest to —

- Ⓐ 200 lb
- Ⓒ 600 lb
- Ⓑ 400 lb
- Ⓓ 1000 lb

20 Use an inch ruler and the map below. What is the actual distance from Appleton to Pearsville?

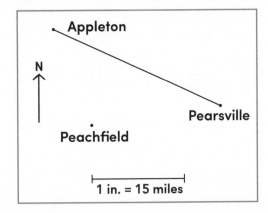

- Ⓐ 75 miles
- Ⓑ 30 miles
- Ⓒ 15 miles
- Ⓓ 2 miles

This bar graph shows the number of days students at Hillview Elementary School missed school each month last year. Use the graph to answer questions 21 and 22.

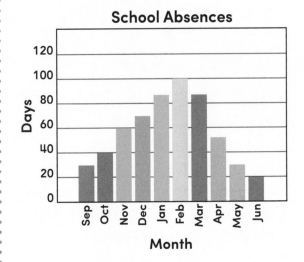

21 In which month were there the fewest absences?

- Ⓐ February
- Ⓑ May
- Ⓒ June
- Ⓓ September

22 About how many days did students miss school in December?

- Ⓐ 40
- Ⓑ 50
- Ⓒ 60
- Ⓓ 70

   © Scholastic Inc.

Answer Sheet

Student Name _____ Grade _____

Teacher Name _____ Date _____

MATHEMATICS

1 Ⓐ Ⓑ Ⓒ Ⓓ Ⓔ	**11** Ⓐ Ⓑ Ⓒ Ⓓ Ⓔ	**21** Ⓐ Ⓑ Ⓒ Ⓓ Ⓔ
2 Ⓐ Ⓑ Ⓒ Ⓓ Ⓔ	**12** Ⓐ Ⓑ Ⓒ Ⓓ Ⓔ	**22** Ⓐ Ⓑ Ⓒ Ⓓ Ⓔ
3 Ⓐ Ⓑ Ⓒ Ⓓ Ⓔ	**13** Ⓐ Ⓑ Ⓒ Ⓓ Ⓔ	**23** Ⓐ Ⓑ Ⓒ Ⓓ Ⓔ
4 Ⓐ Ⓑ Ⓒ Ⓓ Ⓔ	**14** Ⓐ Ⓑ Ⓒ Ⓓ Ⓔ	**24** Ⓐ Ⓑ Ⓒ Ⓓ Ⓔ
5 Ⓐ Ⓑ Ⓒ Ⓓ Ⓔ	**15** Ⓐ Ⓑ Ⓒ Ⓓ Ⓔ	**25** Ⓐ Ⓑ Ⓒ Ⓓ Ⓔ
6 Ⓐ Ⓑ Ⓒ Ⓓ Ⓔ	**16** Ⓐ Ⓑ Ⓒ Ⓓ Ⓔ	**26** Ⓐ Ⓑ Ⓒ Ⓓ Ⓔ
7 Ⓐ Ⓑ Ⓒ Ⓓ Ⓔ	**17** Ⓐ Ⓑ Ⓒ Ⓓ Ⓔ	**27** Ⓐ Ⓑ Ⓒ Ⓓ Ⓔ
8 Ⓐ Ⓑ Ⓒ Ⓓ Ⓔ	**18** Ⓐ Ⓑ Ⓒ Ⓓ Ⓔ	**28** Ⓐ Ⓑ Ⓒ Ⓓ Ⓔ
9 Ⓐ Ⓑ Ⓒ Ⓓ Ⓔ	**19** Ⓐ Ⓑ Ⓒ Ⓓ Ⓔ	**29** Ⓐ Ⓑ Ⓒ Ⓓ Ⓔ
10 Ⓐ Ⓑ Ⓒ Ⓓ Ⓔ	**20** Ⓐ Ⓑ Ⓒ Ⓓ Ⓔ	**30** Ⓐ Ⓑ Ⓒ Ⓓ Ⓔ

Practice Test 3: Problem Solving

Directions. Choose the best answer to each question. Mark your answer. If the correct answer is *not given*, choose "NG."

1 Each bookshelf for a school book fair holds 12 books. How many shelves will be needed to display 75 books?

Ⓐ 6

Ⓑ 7

Ⓒ 63

Ⓓ 87

Ⓔ NG

2 There are 40 sweet wafers in a roll

How many wafers are in the tin?

Ⓐ 63 wafers

Ⓑ 92 wafers

Ⓒ 812 wafers

Ⓓ 920 wafers

Ⓔ NG

3 Tawana is making costumes for the school play. She has $4\frac{3}{8}$ yards of fabric. The pattern calls for $3\frac{1}{4}$ yards of fabric. How much fabric will be left over?

Ⓐ $1\frac{1}{8}$ yards

Ⓑ $1\frac{1}{4}$ yards

Ⓒ $1\frac{1}{2}$ yards

Ⓓ $7\frac{5}{8}$ yards

Ⓔ NG

4 Dave wants to buy a package of baseball cards that costs $3.75. If he saves $0.80 each week, how long will it take him to save enough money for the cards?

Ⓐ 4 weeks

Ⓑ 5 weeks

Ⓒ 6 weeks

Ⓓ 7 weeks

Ⓔ NG

5 Peter's family drove 171 miles in 3 hours. At the same rate, how far will they travel in 10 hours?

Ⓐ 399 miles

Ⓑ 480 miles

Ⓒ 520 miles

Ⓓ 640 miles

Ⓔ NG

GO ON

    © Scholastic Inc.

Practice Test 3 *(continued)*

6 The Social Committee spent $6.98 on paper goods, $9.32 on beverages, $13.04 on snacks, and $7 for decorations for the end-of-year party. How much did the committee spend in all?

Ⓐ $36.34

Ⓑ $35.24

Ⓒ $29.41

Ⓓ $17.71

Ⓔ NG

7 Linda kept track of the time she spent on her science fair project over four days.

Day	Time Spent
Monday	45 minutes
Tuesday	1 hour, 10 min.
Wednesday	24 minutes
Thursday	$1\frac{1}{2}$ hours

How much time did Linda spend on her project all together?

Ⓐ 2 hours, 47 minutes

Ⓑ 3 hours, 7 minutes

Ⓒ 3 hours, 27 minutes

Ⓓ 3 hours, 49 minutes

Ⓔ NG

8 Mr. Addison has 43 fence panels. Each one is 8 feet long. What is the longest fence Mr. Addison can build?

Ⓐ 51 feet

Ⓑ 172 feet

Ⓒ 324 feet

Ⓓ 344 feet

Ⓔ NG

9 There are 20,243 students in a school district. Of them, 1821 students get to school by walking or by bicycle. The rest take the school buses. <u>About</u> how many students take the buses?

Ⓐ 18,000   Ⓒ 20,000

Ⓑ 19,000   Ⓓ 22,000

10 A car powered by electricity and gasoline travels 68 miles per gallon of gasoline. Its tank holds 10.6 gallons of gas. <u>About</u> how far can the car go on a full tank of gas?

Ⓐ 7 miles   Ⓒ 700 miles

Ⓑ 70 miles   Ⓓ 7000 miles

11 The 20 members of the soccer team voted on a new mascot. Three fifths of them voted for the gazelle. How many votes were for the gazelle?

Ⓐ 4 votes

Ⓑ 12 votes

Ⓒ 15 votes

Ⓓ 33 votes

Ⓔ NG

GO ON

Practice Test 3 *(continued)*

12 A map has a scale in which 2.5 cm represents 15 miles. What does 4 cm represent on the map?

Ⓐ 6 miles
Ⓑ 10 miles
Ⓒ 24 miles
Ⓓ 30 miles
Ⓔ NG

13 Five people are standing in a line at the video store. Pete is at the front of the line. Stan is directly in front of Brad. Alison is between Stan and Barb. Who is last in line?

Ⓐ Alison
Ⓑ Stan
Ⓒ Barb
Ⓓ Brad
Ⓔ NG

14 Jed is planning his weekly radio show. There are 7 minutes left in the program. Along with the first track of the featured artist, which track should Jed play to fill the time without going over 7 minutes?

Ⓐ Track 2
Ⓑ Track 3
Ⓒ Track 4
Ⓓ Track 5
Ⓔ NG

Track	Time
1	4:21
2	3:06
3	2:35
4	3:15
5	3:03
6	3:20

Use the chart for questions 15 and 16.

Kendra designed a race track for marbles. She pours her marbles through a funnel onto the track.

Color	Number of Marbles
Green	5
Blue	7
Red	2
Purple	6

15 Which color marble is most likely to win?

Ⓐ green
Ⓑ blue
Ⓒ red
Ⓓ purple

16 What is the probability of a red marble finishing first?

Ⓐ $\frac{1}{5}$
Ⓑ $\frac{1}{10}$
Ⓒ $\frac{1}{4}$
Ⓓ $\frac{1}{8}$
Ⓔ NG

GO ON

© Scholastic Inc.

Practice Test 3 *(continued)*

17 A total of 300 tickets for a door prize were passed out. Mr. Ryan got 6 tickets. What is the probability that one of Mr. Ryan's tickets will be drawn for the prize?

Ⓐ $\frac{50}{1}$

Ⓑ $\frac{3}{25}$

Ⓒ $\frac{1}{50}$

Ⓓ $\frac{1}{300}$

Ⓔ NG

18 It takes Julie $1\frac{2}{3}$ hours to make a gecko with beads. Which number sentence could be used to find how many geckos Julie can make in 15 hours?

Ⓐ $15 \div 1\frac{2}{3} = \square$

Ⓑ $15 + 1\frac{2}{3} = \square$

Ⓒ $15 \times 1\frac{2}{3} = \square$

Ⓓ $15 - 1\frac{2}{3} = \square$

Ⓔ NG

19 Kara plans to paint a wall that is 20 feet long and 9 feet high. There is a 3 ft. by 7 ft. door in the wall. Which number sentence could be used to find the area of the wall to be painted?

Ⓐ $(20 \times 9) - (3 \times 7) = \square$

Ⓑ $(20 \times 9) - 3 - 7 = \square$

Ⓒ $20 \times 9 = \square$

Ⓓ $(20 \times 9) + (3 \times 7) = \square$

Ⓔ NG

20 Ralph bicycled 15 miles on Friday, 22 miles on Saturday, and 17 miles on Sunday. Which number sentence could be used to find the average number of miles he bicycled each day?

Ⓐ $15 + 22 + 17 = \square$

Ⓑ $22 - 17 = \square$

Ⓒ $(15 + 22 + 17) \times 3 = \square$

Ⓓ $(15 + 22 + 17) - 3 = \square$

Ⓔ NG

21 Olivia put $35.75 in a new savings account. The bank pays 6% interest each year. What information do you need to figure out how much money is in Olivia's account now?

Ⓐ how long the money has been in the account

Ⓑ the type of bank she used

Ⓒ the name of the bank

Ⓓ the savings account number

Ⓔ NG

22 A camel can hold 22 gallons of water in its stomachs. Each pint of water weighs 1 pound. How many pounds of water can the camel hold?

Ⓐ 44 lb

Ⓑ 88 lb

Ⓒ 176 lb

Ⓓ 352 lb

Ⓔ NG

STOP

Answer Sheet

Student Name _____   Grade _____

Teacher Name _____   Date _____

MATHEMATICS

1 Ⓐ Ⓑ Ⓒ Ⓓ Ⓔ	**11** Ⓐ Ⓑ Ⓒ Ⓓ Ⓔ	**21** Ⓐ Ⓑ Ⓒ Ⓓ Ⓔ
2 Ⓐ Ⓑ Ⓒ Ⓓ Ⓔ	**12** Ⓐ Ⓑ Ⓒ Ⓓ Ⓔ	**22** Ⓐ Ⓑ Ⓒ Ⓓ Ⓔ
3 Ⓐ Ⓑ Ⓒ Ⓓ Ⓔ	**13** Ⓐ Ⓑ Ⓒ Ⓓ Ⓔ	**23** Ⓐ Ⓑ Ⓒ Ⓓ Ⓔ
4 Ⓐ Ⓑ Ⓒ Ⓓ Ⓔ	**14** Ⓐ Ⓑ Ⓒ Ⓓ Ⓔ	**24** Ⓐ Ⓑ Ⓒ Ⓓ Ⓔ
5 Ⓐ Ⓑ Ⓒ Ⓓ Ⓔ	**15** Ⓐ Ⓑ Ⓒ Ⓓ Ⓔ	**25** Ⓐ Ⓑ Ⓒ Ⓓ Ⓔ
6 Ⓐ Ⓑ Ⓒ Ⓓ Ⓔ	**16** Ⓐ Ⓑ Ⓒ Ⓓ Ⓔ	**26** Ⓐ Ⓑ Ⓒ Ⓓ Ⓔ
7 Ⓐ Ⓑ Ⓒ Ⓓ Ⓔ	**17** Ⓐ Ⓑ Ⓒ Ⓓ Ⓔ	**27** Ⓐ Ⓑ Ⓒ Ⓓ Ⓔ
8 Ⓐ Ⓑ Ⓒ Ⓓ Ⓔ	**18** Ⓐ Ⓑ Ⓒ Ⓓ Ⓔ	**28** Ⓐ Ⓑ Ⓒ Ⓓ Ⓔ
9 Ⓐ Ⓑ Ⓒ Ⓓ Ⓔ	**19** Ⓐ Ⓑ Ⓒ Ⓓ Ⓔ	**29** Ⓐ Ⓑ Ⓒ Ⓓ Ⓔ
10 Ⓐ Ⓑ Ⓒ Ⓓ Ⓔ	**20** Ⓐ Ⓑ Ⓒ Ⓓ Ⓔ	**30** Ⓐ Ⓑ Ⓒ Ⓓ Ⓔ

© Scholastic Inc.

Practice Test 4: Computation

Directions. Choose the best answer to each question. Mark your answer.
If the correct answer is *not given*, choose "NG."

1
$$\begin{array}{r} 40 \\ \times\ 27 \\ \end{array}$$

Ⓐ 360
Ⓑ 828
Ⓒ 1010
Ⓓ 1080
Ⓔ NG

2 $15\overline{)620}$

Ⓐ 42 R5
Ⓑ 41 R5
Ⓒ 41 R3
Ⓓ 40 R5
Ⓔ NG

3 This chart shows the number of movie tickets sold at the theater each day.

Movie Tickets Sold	
Monday	12
Tuesday	20
Wednesday	28
Thursday	36
Friday	54

What was the average number of tickets sold per day?

Ⓐ 150
Ⓑ 37
Ⓒ 30
Ⓓ 28
Ⓔ NG

4 Amy bought 8 boxes of tiles.

How many tiles did she buy in all?

Ⓐ 116
Ⓑ 816
Ⓒ 860
Ⓓ 1864
Ⓔ NG

5
$$\begin{array}{r} \frac{3}{5} \\ +\ \frac{4}{5} \\ \end{array}$$

Ⓐ $\frac{7}{25}$
Ⓑ $1\frac{2}{5}$
Ⓒ $\frac{5}{7}$
Ⓓ $\frac{12}{20}$
Ⓔ NG

6 $\frac{5}{9} - \frac{2}{9} =$

Ⓐ $\frac{7}{9}$
Ⓑ $\frac{10}{18}$
Ⓒ $\frac{3}{18}$
Ⓓ $\frac{2}{3}$
Ⓔ NG

GO ON ▷

Practice Test 4 *(continued)*

7 $\frac{3}{4} - \frac{1}{3} =$

Ⓐ $\frac{5}{12}$

Ⓑ $\frac{1}{2}$

Ⓒ $\frac{3}{7}$

Ⓓ $\frac{1}{4}$

Ⓔ NG

8 Lara is playing a game with letter tiles. These tiles are in a box.

Letter	Number of Tiles
E	12
T	6
A	4
R	8

If Lara takes out one tile without looking, what is the probability that she will get a "T"?

Ⓐ $\frac{4}{5}$

Ⓑ $\frac{1}{4}$

Ⓒ $\frac{3}{10}$

Ⓓ $\frac{1}{5}$

Ⓔ NG

9 $\frac{4}{5} \times \frac{2}{3} =$

Ⓐ $\frac{8}{15}$

Ⓑ $\frac{6}{8}$

Ⓒ $\frac{6}{15}$

Ⓓ $\frac{8}{8}$

Ⓔ NG

10 $\frac{3}{10} \times \frac{1}{2} =$

Ⓐ $\frac{3}{12}$

Ⓑ $\frac{4}{12}$

Ⓒ $\frac{2}{20}$

Ⓓ $\frac{4}{20}$

Ⓔ NG

11
$$\begin{array}{r} \$15.95 \\ +\ 6.28 \\ \hline \end{array}$$

Ⓐ $20.23

Ⓑ $21.13

Ⓒ $22.13

Ⓓ $22.23

Ⓔ NG

12 This chart shows the number of miles Trevor rode his bike each day.

Miles Trevor Rode	
Monday	45
Tuesday	40
Wednesday	32
Thursday	38
Friday	35

What was the average number of miles he rode per day?

Ⓐ 28

Ⓑ 32

Ⓒ 38

Ⓓ 190

Ⓔ NG

GO ON

© Scholastic Inc.

Practice Test 4 *(continued)*

Use the grid map below to answer questions 13 and 14.

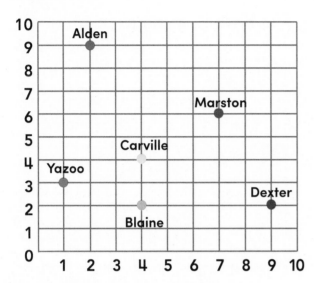

13 **What city is located at (4, 2)?**

Ⓐ Blaine

Ⓑ Yazoo

Ⓒ Carville

Ⓓ Dexter

Ⓔ NG

14 **Where is Marston located?**

Ⓐ (9, 2)

Ⓑ (7, 6)

Ⓒ (4, 4)

Ⓓ (6, 7)

Ⓔ NG

15 1.84 + 2.3 =

Ⓐ 3.14

Ⓑ 3.87

Ⓒ 4.04

Ⓓ 4.24

Ⓔ NG

16 6.3 − 0.8 =

Ⓐ 7.1

Ⓑ 6.5

Ⓒ 5.6

Ⓓ 4.5

Ⓔ NG

17 $20 − $8.95 =

Ⓐ $12.05

Ⓑ $11.05

Ⓒ $10.95

Ⓓ $10.50

Ⓔ NG

18 3.2 × 0.5 =

Ⓐ 0.3

Ⓑ 1.5

Ⓒ 1.6

Ⓓ 16

Ⓔ NG

19 25 × $2.40 =

Ⓐ $6.00

Ⓑ $15.00

Ⓒ $51.00

Ⓓ $60.00

Ⓔ NG

Practice Test 4 *(continued)*

20 Marlo wrote this number sentence to solve a problem.

$$(6 \times 2n) \div 8 = 15$$

What is the value of *n*?

Ⓐ 8

Ⓑ 9

Ⓒ 10

Ⓓ 15

Ⓔ NG

21 If $(3x + 5x) - 4 = 36$, then what is the value of *x*?

Ⓐ 8

Ⓑ 5

Ⓒ 4

Ⓓ 3

Ⓔ NG

22 Collin wrote this equation to solve a problem.

$$7y - 5 = 58$$

What is the value of *y*?

Ⓐ 5

Ⓑ 6

Ⓒ 7

Ⓓ 8

Ⓔ NG

Use the grid below to answer questions 23 and 24.

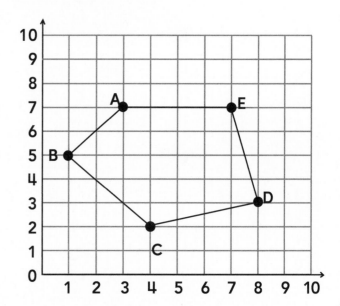

23 What are the coordinates for the location of point D?

Ⓐ (3, 8)

Ⓑ (4, 2)

Ⓒ (4, 4)

Ⓓ (8, 3)

Ⓔ NG

24 Which point is located at (3, 7)?

Ⓐ point A

Ⓑ point B

Ⓒ point C

Ⓓ point E

Ⓔ NG

STOP

© Scholastic Inc.

Answer Sheet

Student Name _____ Grade _____

Teacher Name _____ Date _____

MATHEMATICS

1 Ⓐ Ⓑ Ⓒ Ⓓ Ⓔ	11 Ⓐ Ⓑ Ⓒ Ⓓ Ⓔ	21 Ⓐ Ⓑ Ⓒ Ⓓ Ⓔ
2 Ⓐ Ⓑ Ⓒ Ⓓ Ⓔ	12 Ⓐ Ⓑ Ⓒ Ⓓ Ⓔ	22 Ⓐ Ⓑ Ⓒ Ⓓ Ⓔ
3 Ⓐ Ⓑ Ⓒ Ⓓ Ⓔ	13 Ⓐ Ⓑ Ⓒ Ⓓ Ⓔ	23 Ⓐ Ⓑ Ⓒ Ⓓ Ⓔ
4 Ⓐ Ⓑ Ⓒ Ⓓ Ⓔ	14 Ⓐ Ⓑ Ⓒ Ⓓ Ⓔ	24 Ⓐ Ⓑ Ⓒ Ⓓ Ⓔ
5 Ⓐ Ⓑ Ⓒ Ⓓ Ⓔ	15 Ⓐ Ⓑ Ⓒ Ⓓ Ⓔ	25 Ⓐ Ⓑ Ⓒ Ⓓ Ⓔ
6 Ⓐ Ⓑ Ⓒ Ⓓ Ⓔ	16 Ⓐ Ⓑ Ⓒ Ⓓ Ⓔ	26 Ⓐ Ⓑ Ⓒ Ⓓ Ⓔ
7 Ⓐ Ⓑ Ⓒ Ⓓ Ⓔ	17 Ⓐ Ⓑ Ⓒ Ⓓ Ⓔ	27 Ⓐ Ⓑ Ⓒ Ⓓ Ⓔ
8 Ⓐ Ⓑ Ⓒ Ⓓ Ⓔ	18 Ⓐ Ⓑ Ⓒ Ⓓ Ⓔ	28 Ⓐ Ⓑ Ⓒ Ⓓ Ⓔ
9 Ⓐ Ⓑ Ⓒ Ⓓ Ⓔ	19 Ⓐ Ⓑ Ⓒ Ⓓ Ⓔ	29 Ⓐ Ⓑ Ⓒ Ⓓ Ⓔ
10 Ⓐ Ⓑ Ⓒ Ⓓ Ⓔ	20 Ⓐ Ⓑ Ⓒ Ⓓ Ⓔ	30 Ⓐ Ⓑ Ⓒ Ⓓ Ⓔ

© Scholastic Inc.

Practice Test 5: Numeration and Number Concepts

Directions. Choose the best answer to each question. Mark your answer.

1 Brazil has an area of about 3,287,000 square miles. How is 3,287,000 written in words?

Ⓐ thirty-two million eight hundred seventy thousand

Ⓑ three million two hundred eighty-seven thousand

Ⓒ three hundred twenty-eight thousand seven hundred

Ⓓ three million two hundred thousand eighty-seven

2 The population of Belize is about three hundred thirty-two thousand. How is this number written as a numeral?

Ⓐ 300,032,000

Ⓑ 300,320

Ⓒ 332,000

Ⓓ 300,032

3 Which is an odd number?

Ⓐ 2060

Ⓑ 7254

Ⓒ 1102

Ⓓ 3481

4 The chart shows the population of four states in 2019.

State	Population
Indiana	6,732,219
Missouri	6,137,428
Tennessee	6,829,174
Washington	7,614,893

Which state has the largest population?

Ⓐ Indiana

Ⓑ Washington

Ⓒ Tennessee

Ⓓ Missouri

5 The chart shows the results of the 2020 presidential election in Pennsylvania.

Candidate	Number of Votes
Biden	3,458,299
Trump	3,377,674
Jorgensen	79,380

Which list shows the candidates in order from the greatest number of votes received to the least?

Ⓐ Biden, Trump, Jorgensen

Ⓑ Biden, Jorgensen, Trump

Ⓒ Jorgensen, Trump, Biden

Ⓓ Trump, Jorgensen, Biden

GO ON

© Scholastic Inc.

Practice Test 5 *(continued)*

6 At its farthest point, the moon is 251,966 miles from Earth. What is that number rounded to the nearest ten thousand miles?

Ⓐ 251,970
Ⓑ 251,900
Ⓒ 252,000
Ⓓ 250,000

7 This sign shows the number of cars sold by a car dealer.

| 1 | 8 | 7 | 9 | 3 | 4 | 5 |

The "9" represents what place value in this number?

Ⓐ hundreds
Ⓑ thousands
Ⓒ ten thousands
Ⓓ hundred thousands

8 70,000 + 400 + 80 =

Ⓐ 70,480
Ⓑ 700,480
Ⓒ 70,048
Ⓓ 7480

9 Last year, Darcy earned $14,685.00. What is that number rounded to the nearest hundred dollars?

Ⓐ $15,000
Ⓑ $14,600
Ⓒ $14,690
Ⓓ $14,700

10 An artist designed this carpet pattern

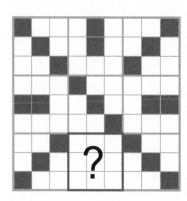

If the pattern continues, what design would fit in the empty block?

Ⓐ   Ⓒ

Ⓑ   Ⓓ

11 The list shows the number of people from three states who visited Niagara Falls.

Pennsylania	6134
Michigan	4288
Ohio	3990

<u>About</u> how many visitors were there all together from these three states?

Ⓐ 12,500
Ⓑ 13,000
Ⓒ 13,500
Ⓓ 14,000

GO ON

Practice Test 5 *(continued)*

12 In a large banquet hall, there are 38 tables. Each table seats 22 people. **About** how many people can be seated in the hall at one time?

(A) 8000　　　　(C) 800

(B) 6000　　　　(D) 600

13 What is the greatest common factor of 9, 12, and 27?

(A) 2　　　　(C) 6

(B) 3　　　　(D) 9

14 What is the least common multiple of 8 and 20?

(A) 4　　　　(C) 80

(B) 40　　　　(D) 160

15 Look at the number line.

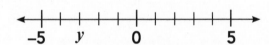

What number belongs in the place marked with *y*?

(A) 3　　　　(C) -2

(B) -1　　　　(D) -3

16 There are 24 students in Ms. Granger's class, and 12 of them are girls. What fraction of the students are girls?

(A) $\frac{1}{2}$　　　　(C) $\frac{3}{5}$

(B) $\frac{1}{3}$　　　　(D) $\frac{2}{3}$

17 Which number line shows the difference of 3 − 5?

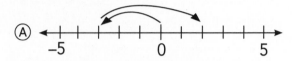

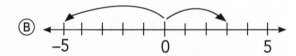

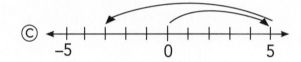

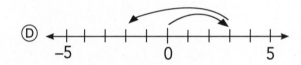

18 $(3x + 1) \times 0 =$

(A) $3x + 1$　　　　(C) 0

(B) $3x + 10$　　　　(D) $1 + 0$

19 Which statement is true?

(A) $9 \times \frac{1}{9} = 1$

(B) $\frac{1}{2} \times \frac{1}{2} = \frac{1}{2} + \frac{1}{2}$

(C) $3 \times \frac{1}{3} = 3$

(D) $\frac{1}{4} \times \frac{1}{4} = \frac{1}{4}$

20 Which of these will result in an even number?

(A) $5 + 7 + 9$　　　　(C) $5 - 3 - 1$

(B) $8 + 0$　　　　(D) $9 - 0$

GO ON ➡

© Scholastic Inc.

Practice Test 5 *(continued)*

21 Which bottle of juice holds the most?

Brand A	$1\frac{1}{2}$ qt
Brand B	$1\frac{3}{4}$ qt
Brand C	$1\frac{2}{3}$ qt
Brand D	$1\frac{5}{6}$ qt

Ⓐ Brand A
Ⓑ Brand B
Ⓒ Brand C
Ⓓ Brand D

22 An oil tank holds 250 gallons. It has 100 gallons of oil in it. What fraction tells how full the tank is?

Ⓐ $\frac{1}{2}$ Ⓒ $\frac{3}{5}$
Ⓑ $\frac{2}{5}$ Ⓓ $\frac{2}{3}$

23 Which decimal number is equal to $\frac{1}{4}$?

Ⓐ 0.20   Ⓒ 0.45
Ⓑ 0.25   Ⓓ 0.50

24 Tino found $0.60. What fraction of a dollar did he find?

Ⓐ $\frac{2}{3}$ Ⓒ $\frac{3}{4}$
Ⓑ $\frac{1}{2}$ Ⓓ $\frac{3}{5}$

25 In a race, four swimmers finished with these times.

James	30.42
Rosa	30.65
Lily	30.33
Rafael	30.71

Which list shows the swimmers in order from fastest time to slowest?

Ⓐ Lily, James, Rosa, Rafael
Ⓑ Rafael, Rosa, James, Lily
Ⓒ Lily, Rosa, Rafael, James
Ⓓ James, Rosa, Rafael, Lily

26 At the grocery store, Mara found four loaves of bread at four different prices. Which is the highest price?

Ⓐ 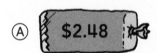 $2.48

Ⓑ  $2.55

Ⓒ  $2.69

Ⓓ  $2.63

STOP

Answer Sheet

Student Name _____ Grade _____

Teacher Name _____ Date _____

MATHEMATICS

1 Ⓐ Ⓑ Ⓒ Ⓓ Ⓔ	**11** Ⓐ Ⓑ Ⓒ Ⓓ Ⓔ	**21** Ⓐ Ⓑ Ⓒ Ⓓ Ⓔ
2 Ⓐ Ⓑ Ⓒ Ⓓ Ⓔ	**12** Ⓐ Ⓑ Ⓒ Ⓓ Ⓔ	**22** Ⓐ Ⓑ Ⓒ Ⓓ Ⓔ
3 Ⓐ Ⓑ Ⓒ Ⓓ Ⓔ	**13** Ⓐ Ⓑ Ⓒ Ⓓ Ⓔ	**23** Ⓐ Ⓑ Ⓒ Ⓓ Ⓔ
4 Ⓐ Ⓑ Ⓒ Ⓓ Ⓔ	**14** Ⓐ Ⓑ Ⓒ Ⓓ Ⓔ	**24** Ⓐ Ⓑ Ⓒ Ⓓ Ⓔ
5 Ⓐ Ⓑ Ⓒ Ⓓ Ⓔ	**15** Ⓐ Ⓑ Ⓒ Ⓓ Ⓔ	**25** Ⓐ Ⓑ Ⓒ Ⓓ Ⓔ
6 Ⓐ Ⓑ Ⓒ Ⓓ Ⓔ	**16** Ⓐ Ⓑ Ⓒ Ⓓ Ⓔ	**26** Ⓐ Ⓑ Ⓒ Ⓓ Ⓔ
7 Ⓐ Ⓑ Ⓒ Ⓓ Ⓔ	**17** Ⓐ Ⓑ Ⓒ Ⓓ Ⓔ	**27** Ⓐ Ⓑ Ⓒ Ⓓ Ⓔ
8 Ⓐ Ⓑ Ⓒ Ⓓ Ⓔ	**18** Ⓐ Ⓑ Ⓒ Ⓓ Ⓔ	**28** Ⓐ Ⓑ Ⓒ Ⓓ Ⓔ
9 Ⓐ Ⓑ Ⓒ Ⓓ Ⓔ	**19** Ⓐ Ⓑ Ⓒ Ⓓ Ⓔ	**29** Ⓐ Ⓑ Ⓒ Ⓓ Ⓔ
10 Ⓐ Ⓑ Ⓒ Ⓓ Ⓔ	**20** Ⓐ Ⓑ Ⓒ Ⓓ Ⓔ	**30** Ⓐ Ⓑ Ⓒ Ⓓ Ⓔ

© Scholastic Inc.

Practice Test 6: Geometry and Measurement

Directions. Choose the best answer to each question. Mark your answer

1 Which figure is a pentagon?

Ⓐ  Ⓒ

Ⓑ Ⓓ

2 Merrill rode 3.5 kilometers on his bike. How many meters is that?

Ⓐ 0.35
Ⓑ 35
Ⓒ 350
Ⓓ 3500

3 Which figure has 5 faces?

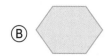

Ⓐ Ⓒ

Ⓑ Ⓓ

4 Which figure shows a line of symmetry?

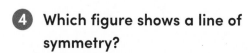

Ⓐ Ⓒ

Ⓑ Ⓓ

5 Suppose that this figure is turned one 90-degree turn in the direction of the arrow.

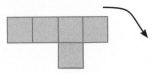

Which picture shows how the figure would look after it has been turned?

Ⓐ

Ⓑ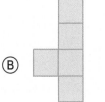

Ⓒ

Ⓓ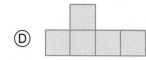

GO ON

© Scholastic Inc.

Practice Test 6 *(continued)*

6 **Look at Figure A**

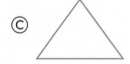

Fig. A

Which is congruent to Figure A?

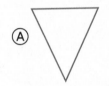

Ⓐ

Ⓒ

Ⓑ

Ⓓ

7 There is a rectangular basketball court at the city playground.

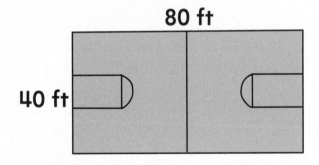

80 ft

40 ft

What is the perimeter of the court?

Ⓐ 120 ft

Ⓑ 200 ft

Ⓒ 240 ft

Ⓓ 3200 ft

Use the picture to answer questions 8 and 9.

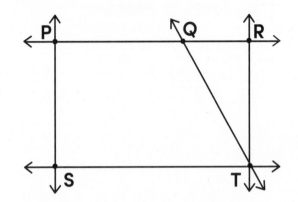

8 **Which line is parallel to $\overleftrightarrow{PR}$?**

Ⓐ $\overleftrightarrow{PS}$

Ⓑ $\overleftrightarrow{QT}$

Ⓒ $\overrightarrow{RT}$

Ⓓ $\overleftrightarrow{ST}$

9 **Which is a right angle?**

Ⓐ ∠TSP

Ⓑ ∠PQT

Ⓒ ∠QTR

Ⓓ ∠RQT

10 Sherman made 3 quarts of lemonade. How many cups did he make?

Ⓐ 6 cups

Ⓑ 9 cups

Ⓒ 12 cups

Ⓓ 24 cups

GO ON

© Scholastic Inc.

Practice Test 6 *(continued)*

11 If you slide figure KLM 2 spaces to the right and 1 space down, what will be the new coordinates of point M?

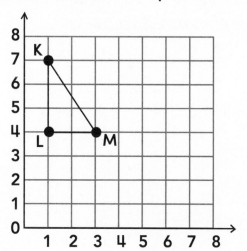

- Ⓐ (3, 4)
- Ⓒ (5, 3)
- Ⓑ (4, 2)
- Ⓓ (3, 3)

12 What is the volume of this tool chest?

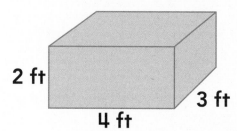

2 ft

3 ft

4 ft

- Ⓐ 9 ft³
- Ⓒ 24 ft³
- Ⓑ 12 ft³
- Ⓓ 48 ft³

13 Which unit should be used to measure the weight of a package of cheese?

- Ⓐ ounces
- Ⓑ inches
- Ⓒ quarts
- Ⓓ feet

14 Maggie went to sleep at 8:30 P.M. Her clock showed this time when she woke up the next morning. How long did she sleep?

- Ⓐ 9 hr, 15 min
- Ⓑ 9 hr, 30 min
- Ⓒ 10 hr, 15 min
- Ⓓ 10 hr, 30 min

15 Cole spent 2 hours and 15 minutes mowing the lawn. He started at 4:30 P.M. What time did he finish?

- Ⓐ 5:45 P.M.
- Ⓒ 6:45 P.M.
- Ⓑ 6:30 P.M.
- Ⓓ 7:00 P.M.

16 Which of these is about 1 meter long?

- Ⓐ a baseball bat
- Ⓑ a pick-up truck
- Ⓒ an egg
- Ⓓ a man's shoe

17 One side of a square sandbox is 7 feet long. What is the area of the sandbox?

- Ⓐ 98 sq ft
- Ⓒ 28 sq ft
- Ⓑ 49 sq ft
- Ⓓ 14 sq ft

18 A bathtub that is filled with water would hold about how many gallons?

- Ⓐ 3 gal
- Ⓒ 300 gal
- Ⓑ 30 gal
- Ⓓ 3000 gal

GO ON

© Scholastic Inc.

Practice Test 6 *(continued)*

Use a centimeter ruler and the map below to answer questions 19 and 20.

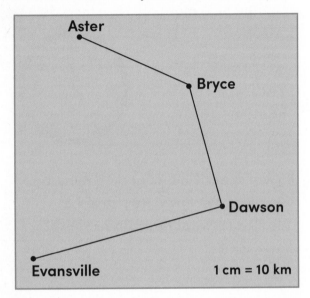

This graph shows the average attendance at hockey games played by the Cougars each month. Use the graph to answer questions 22–24.

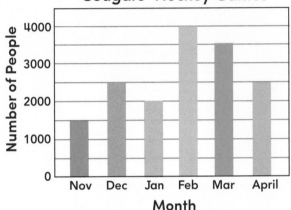

19 What is the actual distance from Aster to Bryce?

Ⓐ 3 km   Ⓒ 30 km

Ⓑ 4 km   Ⓓ 40 km

20 Lanny drove from Bryce to Dawson to Evansville. How far did he drive in all?

Ⓐ 8 km   Ⓒ 70 km

Ⓑ 60 km   Ⓓ 80 km

21 There are 20 fifth graders on a school bus. All together, these 20 students probably weigh about —

Ⓐ 300–500 lb

Ⓑ 600–800 lb

Ⓒ 900–1100 lb

Ⓓ 1400–1600 lb

22 In which month was the average attendance highest?

Ⓐ December   Ⓒ March

Ⓑ January   Ⓓ February

23 What was the average attendance in April?

Ⓐ 1500   Ⓒ 2500

Ⓑ 2000   Ⓓ 3000

24 What was the difference in average attendance between November and December?

Ⓐ 1000   Ⓒ 2000

Ⓑ 1500   Ⓓ 2500

    © Scholastic Inc.

Answer Sheet

Student Name _____ Grade _____

Teacher Name _____ Date _____

MATHEMATICS

1 Ⓐ Ⓑ Ⓒ Ⓓ Ⓔ	11 Ⓐ Ⓑ Ⓒ Ⓓ Ⓔ	21 Ⓐ Ⓑ Ⓒ Ⓓ Ⓔ
2 Ⓐ Ⓑ Ⓒ Ⓓ Ⓔ	12 Ⓐ Ⓑ Ⓒ Ⓓ Ⓔ	22 Ⓐ Ⓑ Ⓒ Ⓓ Ⓔ
3 Ⓐ Ⓑ Ⓒ Ⓓ Ⓔ	13 Ⓐ Ⓑ Ⓒ Ⓓ Ⓔ	23 Ⓐ Ⓑ Ⓒ Ⓓ Ⓔ
4 Ⓐ Ⓑ Ⓒ Ⓓ Ⓔ	14 Ⓐ Ⓑ Ⓒ Ⓓ Ⓔ	24 Ⓐ Ⓑ Ⓒ Ⓓ Ⓔ
5 Ⓐ Ⓑ Ⓒ Ⓓ Ⓔ	15 Ⓐ Ⓑ Ⓒ Ⓓ Ⓔ	25 Ⓐ Ⓑ Ⓒ Ⓓ Ⓔ
6 Ⓐ Ⓑ Ⓒ Ⓓ Ⓔ	16 Ⓐ Ⓑ Ⓒ Ⓓ Ⓔ	26 Ⓐ Ⓑ Ⓒ Ⓓ Ⓔ
7 Ⓐ Ⓑ Ⓒ Ⓓ Ⓔ	17 Ⓐ Ⓑ Ⓒ Ⓓ Ⓔ	27 Ⓐ Ⓑ Ⓒ Ⓓ Ⓔ
8 Ⓐ Ⓑ Ⓒ Ⓓ Ⓔ	18 Ⓐ Ⓑ Ⓒ Ⓓ Ⓔ	28 Ⓐ Ⓑ Ⓒ Ⓓ Ⓔ
9 Ⓐ Ⓑ Ⓒ Ⓓ Ⓔ	19 Ⓐ Ⓑ Ⓒ Ⓓ Ⓔ	29 Ⓐ Ⓑ Ⓒ Ⓓ Ⓔ
10 Ⓐ Ⓑ Ⓒ Ⓓ Ⓔ	20 Ⓐ Ⓑ Ⓒ Ⓓ Ⓔ	30 Ⓐ Ⓑ Ⓒ Ⓓ Ⓔ

© Scholastic Inc.

Practice Test 7: Problem Solving

Directions. Choose the best answer to each question. Mark your answer. If the correct answer is *not given*, choose "NG."

1 A restaurant owner puts 7 rolls in a basket for each table. She has baked 135 rolls. What is the greatest number of baskets she can fill?

Ⓐ 17
Ⓑ 18
Ⓒ 19
Ⓓ 20
Ⓔ NG

2 Fred bought 25 pounds of roofing nails.

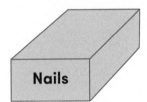

Nails

1 pound = 80 nails

How many nails did he buy in all?

Ⓐ 105
Ⓑ 190
Ⓒ 1600
Ⓓ 2000
Ⓔ NG

3 An average of 3160 cars cross the Gulf Bridge every hour. <u>About</u> how many cars cross the bridge every 12 hours?

Ⓐ 3600   Ⓒ 24,000
Ⓑ 6000   Ⓓ 36,000

4 In the town of Acton, the bike path is $5\frac{1}{2}$ miles long. The hiking trail is $3\frac{3}{4}$ miles long. How much longer is the bike path than the hiking trail?

Ⓐ $\frac{3}{4}$ mile
Ⓑ $1\frac{1}{4}$ miles
Ⓒ $1\frac{1}{2}$ miles
Ⓓ $2\frac{3}{4}$ miles
Ⓔ NG

5 Coach Anders ordered 14 hats for the baseball team. The total cost for the hats was $110.60. How much did each hat cost?

Ⓐ $6.80
Ⓑ $7.90
Ⓒ $124.60
Ⓓ $1548.40
Ⓔ NG

6 Mrs. Jackson spent $2.79 for orange juice, $13.55 for tuna fish, and $8.90 for bread. How much did she spend in all?

Ⓐ $22.45
Ⓑ $23.32
Ⓒ $24.24
Ⓓ $25.84
Ⓔ NG

GO ON

  © Scholastic Inc.

Practice Test 7 *(continued)*

7 The card shows how many hours Romy worked each day.

Day	Hours
Thursday	4.25
Friday	6.50
Saturday	11.50
Sunday	9.00

How many hours did she work in all?

Ⓐ 30.25 hr

Ⓑ 30.75 hr

Ⓒ 31.25 hr

Ⓓ 32.35 hr

Ⓔ NG

8 At the factory, Marco packs 10.4 pounds of shrimp in each crate. <u>About</u> how many pounds of shrimp are in 32 crates?

Ⓐ 3 lb

Ⓑ 30 lb

Ⓒ 300 lb

Ⓓ 3000 lb

9 In a state park that covers a total of 19,880 acres of land, 4910 acres are open for camping. <u>About</u> how many acres are not open for camping?

Ⓐ 4000 acres

Ⓑ 5000 acres

Ⓒ 14,000 acres

Ⓓ 15,000 acres

10 Of the 72 students in the school band, $\frac{3}{4}$ are boys. How many band members are boys?

Ⓐ 18

Ⓑ 48

Ⓒ 54

Ⓓ 60

Ⓔ NG

11 According to the scale on a map, $\frac{1}{2}$ inch represents 25 miles. What does 2 inches represent?

Ⓐ $12\frac{1}{2}$ miles

Ⓑ 50 miles

Ⓒ 60 miles

Ⓓ 75 miles

Ⓔ NG

12 Ramon ordered these items from a catalog.

> 2 posters @ $15.00 each
> 3 books @ $4.50 each
> 1 comic @ $6.25

What was the total cost of these items (not including tax)?

Ⓐ $34.75

Ⓑ $33.25

Ⓒ $28.50

Ⓓ $24.75

Ⓔ NG

GO ON ⟹

Practice Test 7 *(continued)*

The chart below shows the number of colored gumballs Greta has in a bag. Use the chart to answer questions 13 and 14.

Color	Number of Gumballs
Red	10
Yellow	4
Green	6
Purple	5
White	5

13 If Greta reaches in and takes one gumball without looking, what color is she most likely to get?

Ⓐ red

Ⓑ yellow

Ⓒ green

Ⓓ white

Ⓔ NG

14 What is the probability that she will pick a purple gumball?

Ⓐ $\frac{3}{10}$

Ⓑ $\frac{1}{5}$

Ⓒ $\frac{1}{4}$

Ⓓ $\frac{1}{6}$

Ⓔ NG

15 Five girls are standing in line at an ice cream shop. Rita is standing in front of Mary Jo and behind Sue. Lin is standing behind Beth but in front of Sue. Who is first in line?

Ⓐ Sue

Ⓑ Lin

Ⓒ Beth

Ⓓ Rita

Ⓔ NG

16 Chuck has 6 coins in his pocket. They are all dimes, nickels, and pennies, and he has at least one of each. What is the greatest amount of money he could have?

Ⓐ $0.34

Ⓑ $0.46

Ⓒ $0.52

Ⓓ $0.60

Ⓔ NG

17 On hiking trips, Jane hikes $1\frac{1}{2}$ miles per hour. Which number sentence could be used to find how far Jane hikes in 6 hours?

Ⓐ $6 \times 1\frac{1}{2} = \square$

Ⓑ $6 + 1\frac{1}{2} = \square$

Ⓒ $6 \div 1\frac{1}{2} = \square$

Ⓓ $6 - 1\frac{1}{2} = \square$

Ⓔ NG

GO ON ➡

© Scholastic Inc.

Practice Test 7 *(continued)*

18 Charles works 12 hours each week as a baby-sitter. What else do you need to know to figure out how many weeks it will take him to earn $300?

Ⓐ how many children he baby-sits

Ⓑ where he goes to baby-sit

Ⓒ which days of the week he works

Ⓓ how much he earns per hour

Ⓔ NG

19 Risa read 40 pages of a book on Monday, 35 pages on Tuesday, and 60 pages on Wednesday. Which number sentence could be used to find the average number of pages she read each day?

Ⓐ $(40 + 35 + 60) \div 4 = \square$

Ⓑ $(40 + 35 + 60) \times 3 = \square$

Ⓒ $(40 + 35 + 60) - 3 = \square$

Ⓓ $40 + 35 + 60 = \square$

Ⓔ NG

20 At the movie theater, tickets cost $7.00 for adults and $5.50 for children. If 25 adults and 10 children go to a movie, how much money will be spent on tickets?

Ⓐ $55.00

Ⓑ $175.00

Ⓒ $225.00

Ⓓ $230.00

Ⓔ NG

21 The table shows how many hours Marco and Tina worked at the church fair on Saturday and Sunday.

	Saturday	Sunday
Marco	$3\frac{1}{2}$	4
Tina	$4\frac{1}{2}$	$2\frac{3}{4}$

How much longer did Marco work?

Ⓐ $\frac{3}{4}$ hour

Ⓑ 1 hour

Ⓒ $1\frac{1}{2}$ hours

Ⓓ $1\frac{3}{4}$ hours

Ⓔ NG

22 Mr. Percy made 30 gallons of maple syrup on his farm. He sells the syrup for $12 per quart. If he sells all the syrup he made, how much money will he earn?

Ⓐ $360

Ⓑ $620

Ⓒ $680

Ⓓ $740

Ⓔ NG

STOP

Answer Sheet

Student Name _____ Grade _____

Teacher Name _____ Date _____

MATHEMATICS

1 Ⓐ Ⓑ Ⓒ Ⓓ Ⓔ	11 Ⓐ Ⓑ Ⓒ Ⓓ Ⓔ	21 Ⓐ Ⓑ Ⓒ Ⓓ Ⓔ
2 Ⓐ Ⓑ Ⓒ Ⓓ Ⓔ	12 Ⓐ Ⓑ Ⓒ Ⓓ Ⓔ	22 Ⓐ Ⓑ Ⓒ Ⓓ Ⓔ
3 Ⓐ Ⓑ Ⓒ Ⓓ Ⓔ	13 Ⓐ Ⓑ Ⓒ Ⓓ Ⓔ	23 Ⓐ Ⓑ Ⓒ Ⓓ Ⓔ
4 Ⓐ Ⓑ Ⓒ Ⓓ Ⓔ	14 Ⓐ Ⓑ Ⓒ Ⓓ Ⓔ	24 Ⓐ Ⓑ Ⓒ Ⓓ Ⓔ
5 Ⓐ Ⓑ Ⓒ Ⓓ Ⓔ	15 Ⓐ Ⓑ Ⓒ Ⓓ Ⓔ	25 Ⓐ Ⓑ Ⓒ Ⓓ Ⓔ
6 Ⓐ Ⓑ Ⓒ Ⓓ Ⓔ	16 Ⓐ Ⓑ Ⓒ Ⓓ Ⓔ	26 Ⓐ Ⓑ Ⓒ Ⓓ Ⓔ
7 Ⓐ Ⓑ Ⓒ Ⓓ Ⓔ	17 Ⓐ Ⓑ Ⓒ Ⓓ Ⓔ	27 Ⓐ Ⓑ Ⓒ Ⓓ Ⓔ
8 Ⓐ Ⓑ Ⓒ Ⓓ Ⓔ	18 Ⓐ Ⓑ Ⓒ Ⓓ Ⓔ	28 Ⓐ Ⓑ Ⓒ Ⓓ Ⓔ
9 Ⓐ Ⓑ Ⓒ Ⓓ Ⓔ	19 Ⓐ Ⓑ Ⓒ Ⓓ Ⓔ	29 Ⓐ Ⓑ Ⓒ Ⓓ Ⓔ
10 Ⓐ Ⓑ Ⓒ Ⓓ Ⓔ	20 Ⓐ Ⓑ Ⓒ Ⓓ Ⓔ	30 Ⓐ Ⓑ Ⓒ Ⓓ Ⓔ

© Scholastic Inc.

Practice Test 8: Computation

Directions. Choose the best answer to each question. Mark your answer.
If the correct answer is *not given*, choose "NG."

1
$$\begin{array}{r} 50 \\ \times\ 39 \\ \hline \end{array}$$

(A) 600
(B) 1930
(C) 1950
(D) 2050
(E) NG

2 $12\overline{)580}$

(A) 46
(B) 46 R4
(C) 48 R2
(D) 48 R4
(E) NG

3 A total of 22 cases of juice boxes were sold at a store.

Juice
1 case   24 boxes

How many juice boxes were sold in all?

(A) 96
(B) 428
(C) 524
(D) 628
(E) NG

4 $\frac{3}{10} + \frac{1}{5} =$

(A) $\frac{4}{15}$
(B) $\frac{2}{5}$
(C) $\frac{3}{5}$
(D) $\frac{1}{2}$
(E) NG

5 $\frac{5}{8} - \frac{3}{8} =$

(A) $\frac{1}{8}$
(B) $\frac{1}{2}$
(C) $\frac{1}{3}$
(D) 2
(E) NG

6 $\frac{2}{3} - \frac{1}{2} =$

(A) $\frac{1}{6}$
(B) $\frac{1}{4}$
(C) $\frac{1}{5}$
(D) $\frac{1}{2}$
(E) NG

7 $3.28 + 4.7 =$

(A) 7.98
(B) 7.35
(C) 7.15
(D) 3.75
(E) NG

GO ON

Practice Test 8 (continued)

8 A deli offers 5 kinds of sandwich meats, 2 kinds of cheese, and 3 kinds of bread.

Deli Sandwiches		
Meats	Cheeses	Breads
5	2	3

How many different combinations of 1 meat, 1 cheese, and 1 bread can be made?

Ⓐ 10
Ⓑ 15
Ⓒ 24
Ⓓ 30
Ⓔ NG

9 At a carnival, these prizes are in a box.

Prize	Number
puppet	8
stuffed animal	10
yo-yo	15
rabbit's foot	7

If you take one prize without looking, what is the probability of getting a stuffed animal?

Ⓐ $\frac{1}{2}$
Ⓑ $\frac{1}{4}$
Ⓒ $\frac{1}{10}$
Ⓓ $\frac{1}{5}$
Ⓔ NG

10 $\frac{1}{3} \times \frac{3}{4} =$

Ⓐ $\frac{4}{12}$
Ⓑ $\frac{3}{7}$
Ⓒ $\frac{1}{4}$
Ⓓ $\frac{2}{3}$
Ⓔ NG

11 $\frac{5}{8} \times \frac{1}{2} =$

Ⓐ $\frac{3}{8}$
Ⓑ $\frac{7}{16}$
Ⓒ $\frac{4}{5}$
Ⓓ $\frac{1}{2}$
Ⓔ NG

12
$$\begin{array}{r} \$16.75 \\ + \quad 4.29 \\ \hline \end{array}$$

Ⓐ $12.46
Ⓑ $20.04
Ⓒ $20.94
Ⓓ $21.04
Ⓔ NG

13 $9.1 - 0.7 =$

Ⓐ 2.1
Ⓑ 8.03
Ⓒ 8.4
Ⓓ 9.8
Ⓔ NG

14 $30 - $12.75 =

Ⓐ $16.25
Ⓑ $17.45
Ⓒ $17.75
Ⓓ $18.25
Ⓔ NG

GO ON

   © Scholastic Inc.

Practice Test 8 *(continued)*

15 $5.6 \times 0.4 =$

Ⓐ 2.24
Ⓑ 5.1
Ⓒ 7.4
Ⓓ 20.24
Ⓔ NG

16 $18 \times \$3.60 =$

Ⓐ $54.80
Ⓑ $60.80
Ⓒ $64.80
Ⓓ $65.80
Ⓔ NG

17 This chart shows the number of new books purchased for the school library each year.

Books Purchased	
2017	40
2018	32
2019	45
2020	18
2021	15

What was the average number of books purchased per year?

Ⓐ 25
Ⓑ 30
Ⓒ 37.5
Ⓓ 150
Ⓔ NG

18 Suki wrote this number sentence to solve a problem.

$$(5 \times 4y) \div 4 = 10$$

What is the value of y?

Ⓐ 2
Ⓑ 3
Ⓒ 4
Ⓓ 5
Ⓔ NG

19 Zoe rolls two number cubes numbered 1–6. What is the probability that she will roll 10 on one try?

Ⓐ $\frac{3}{35}$
Ⓑ $\frac{1}{12}$
Ⓒ $\frac{1}{10}$
Ⓓ $\frac{4}{9}$
Ⓔ NG

20 If $(7x + 4x) - 13 = 20$, then what is the value of x?

Ⓐ 2
Ⓑ 3
Ⓒ 5
Ⓓ 6
Ⓔ NG

GO ON

Practice Test 8 *(continued)*

21 Hector wrote this equation to solve a problem.

$$5a - 8 = 37$$

What is the value of *a*?

Ⓐ 6

Ⓑ 7

Ⓒ 8

Ⓓ 9

Ⓔ NG

22 $7\overline{)94}$

Ⓐ 14 R3

Ⓑ 13 R3

Ⓒ 13 R4

Ⓓ 12 R3

Ⓔ NG

23 $\dfrac{5}{5} + \dfrac{5}{6} =$

Ⓐ $1\dfrac{2}{3}$

Ⓑ $\dfrac{10}{12}$

Ⓒ $1\dfrac{3}{6}$

Ⓓ $\dfrac{10}{36}$

Ⓔ NG

Use the grid below to answer questions 24 and 25.

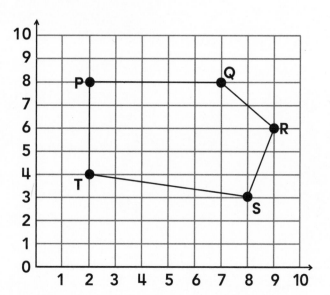

24 **What are the coordinates for the location of point R?**

Ⓐ (2, 8)

Ⓑ (8, 3)

Ⓒ (8, 6)

Ⓓ (9, 6)

Ⓔ NG

25 **Which point is located at (7, 8)?**

Ⓐ P

Ⓑ Q

Ⓒ R

Ⓓ S

Ⓔ NG

STOP

© Scholastic Inc.

Answer Sheet

Student Name _____   Grade _____

Teacher Name _____   Date _____

MATHEMATICS

1 Ⓐ Ⓑ Ⓒ Ⓓ Ⓔ	11 Ⓐ Ⓑ Ⓒ Ⓓ Ⓔ	21 Ⓐ Ⓑ Ⓒ Ⓓ Ⓔ
2 Ⓐ Ⓑ Ⓒ Ⓓ Ⓔ	12 Ⓐ Ⓑ Ⓒ Ⓓ Ⓔ	22 Ⓐ Ⓑ Ⓒ Ⓓ Ⓔ
3 Ⓐ Ⓑ Ⓒ Ⓓ Ⓔ	13 Ⓐ Ⓑ Ⓒ Ⓓ Ⓔ	23 Ⓐ Ⓑ Ⓒ Ⓓ Ⓔ
4 Ⓐ Ⓑ Ⓒ Ⓓ Ⓔ	14 Ⓐ Ⓑ Ⓒ Ⓓ Ⓔ	24 Ⓐ Ⓑ Ⓒ Ⓓ Ⓔ
5 Ⓐ Ⓑ Ⓒ Ⓓ Ⓔ	15 Ⓐ Ⓑ Ⓒ Ⓓ Ⓔ	25 Ⓐ Ⓑ Ⓒ Ⓓ Ⓔ
6 Ⓐ Ⓑ Ⓒ Ⓓ Ⓔ	16 Ⓐ Ⓑ Ⓒ Ⓓ Ⓔ	26 Ⓐ Ⓑ Ⓒ Ⓓ Ⓔ
7 Ⓐ Ⓑ Ⓒ Ⓓ Ⓔ	17 Ⓐ Ⓑ Ⓒ Ⓓ Ⓔ	27 Ⓐ Ⓑ Ⓒ Ⓓ Ⓔ
8 Ⓐ Ⓑ Ⓒ Ⓓ Ⓔ	18 Ⓐ Ⓑ Ⓒ Ⓓ Ⓔ	28 Ⓐ Ⓑ Ⓒ Ⓓ Ⓔ
9 Ⓐ Ⓑ Ⓒ Ⓓ Ⓔ	19 Ⓐ Ⓑ Ⓒ Ⓓ Ⓔ	29 Ⓐ Ⓑ Ⓒ Ⓓ Ⓔ
10 Ⓐ Ⓑ Ⓒ Ⓓ Ⓔ	20 Ⓐ Ⓑ Ⓒ Ⓓ Ⓔ	30 Ⓐ Ⓑ Ⓒ Ⓓ Ⓔ

© Scholastic Inc.

TESTED SKILLS

Practice Test 1: Numeration and Number Concepts

Tested Skills	Item Numbers
Associate numerals and number words	1, 2
Compare and order whole numbers	4, 6
Use place value and rounding	3, 5, 7
Identify patterns (visual, number, odd/even)	8, 9
Estimation	10, 12
Factoring (including GCF) and multiples	13, 14
Identify fractional parts	17, 18
Compare and order fractions (including equivalent)	19, 20
Convert fractions and decimals	21, 22
Compare and order decimals	23, 24
Use number lines (with decimals, fractions, or integers)	15, 16
Apply operational properties	11, 25

Practice Test 2: Geometry and Measurement

Tested Skills	Item Numbers
Identify parts and characteristics of plane and solid figures	1, 7
Recognize symmetry and congruence	3, 6
Identify points, lines, line segments, angles	8, 9
Identify transformations	10, 11
Find perimeter, area, and volume	4, 12, 13
Find elapsed time	14, 15
Use appropriate units of measurement	16, 17
Convert units of measure (standard, metric)	2, 18
Estimate measurements	19
Use scale to determine distance	20
Interpret bar graphs, pictographs, line graphs, tables, charts	5, 21, 22

Practice Test 3: Problem Solving

Tested Skills	Item Numbers
Solve one-step problems using basic operations	1, 2, 3
Solve problems involving money, time, measurement	4, 6, 7, 8
Solve problems involving estimation and ratio/proportion	5, 9, 10, 11, 12
Solve problems involving probability or logic	13, 14, 15, 16, 17
Identify steps in solving problems	18, 19, 20, 21
Solve multi-step problems	22

Practice Test 4: Computation

Tested Skills	Item Numbers
Compute with whole numbers	1, 2, 4
Add and subtract fractions	5, 6, 7
Multiply fractions	9, 10
Add and subtract decimals	11, 15, 16, 17
Multiply decimals	18, 19
Find average, probability, and combinations	3, 8, 12
Solve simple equations	20, 21, 22
Plot points on a coordinate graph	13, 14, 23, 24

© Scholastic Inc.

Practice Test 5: Numeration and Number Concepts

Tested Skills	Item Numbers
Associate numerals and number words	1, 2
Compare and order whole numbers	4, 5
Use place value and rounding	6, 7, 8, 9
Identify patterns	3, 10, 20
Estimation	11, 12
Factoring and multiples	13, 14
Identify fractional parts	16, 22
Compare and order fractions and decimals	21, 25, 26
Convert fractions and decimals	23
Use number lines (with decimals, fractions, or images)	15, 17, 24
Apply operational properties	18, 19

Practice Test 6: Geometry and Measurement

Tested Skills	Item Numbers
Identify parts and characteristics of plane and solid figures	1, 3
Recognize symmetry and congruence	4, 6
Identify points, lines, line segments, angles	8, 9
Identify transformations	5, 11
Find perimeter, area, and volume	7, 12, 17
Find elapsed time	14, 15
Use appropriate units of measurement	2, 10, 13, 16
Estimate measurements	18, 21
Use scale to determine distance	19, 20
Interpret graphs, tables, charts	22, 23, 24

Practice Test 7: Problem Solving

Tested Skills	Item Numbers
Solve one-step problems using basic operations	1, 2, 4
Solve problems involving money, time, measurement	5, 6, 7
Solve problems involving estimation and ratio/proportion	3, 8, 9, 10, 11
Solve problems involving probability or logic	13, 14, 15, 16
Identify steps in solving problems	17, 18, 19
Solve multi-step problems	12, 20, 21, 22

Practice Test 8: Computation

Tested Skills	Item Numbers
Compute with whole numbers	1, 2, 3, 22
Add and subtract fractions	4, 5, 6, 23
Multiply fractions	10, 11
Add and subtract decimals	7, 12, 13, 14
Multiply decimals	15, 16
Find average, probability, and combinations	8, 9, 17, 19
Solve simple equations	18, 20, 21
Plot points on a coordinate graph	24, 25

© Scholastic Inc.

ANSWER KEYS

Practice Test 1
Numeration and Number Concepts

1. C		14. B	
2. A		15. C	
3. A		16. B	
4. D		17. C	
5. C		18. D	
6. B		19. D	
7. D		20. C	
8. B		21. B	
9. C		22. D	
10. A		23. A	
11. A		24. A	
12. A		25. D	
13. B			

Practice Test 2
Geometry and Measurement

1. B		12. C	
2. D		13. C	
3. A		14. A	
4. C		15. B	
5. D		16. D	
6. B		17. C	
7. D		18. A	
8. C		19. D	
9. B		20. B	
10. D		21. C	
11. D		22. D	

Practice Test 3
Problem Solving

1. B		12. C	
2. D		13. D	
3. A		14. B	
4. B		15. B	
5. E		16. B	
6. A		17. C	
7. D		18. A	
8. D		19. A	
9. A		20. E	
10. C		21. A	
11. B		22. C	

Practice Test 4
Computation

1. D		13. A	
2. B		14. B	
3. C		15. E	
4. E		16. E	
5. B		17. B	
6. E		18. C	
7. A		19. D	
8. D		20. C	
9. A		21. B	
10. C		22. E	
11. D		23. D	
12. C		24. A	

Practice Test 5
Numeration and Number Concepts

1. B		14. B	
2. C		15. D	
3. D		16. A	
4. B		17. D	
5. A		18. C	
6. D		19. A	
7. B		20. B	
8. A		21. D	
9. D		22. B	
10. A		23. B	
11. D		24. D	
12. C		25. A	
13. B		26. A	

Practice Test 6
Geometry and Measurement

1. D		13. A	
2. D		14. D	
3. B		15. C	
4. A		16. A	
5. B		17. B	
6. B		18. B	
7. C		19. C	
8. D		20. D	
9. A		21. D	
10. C		22. D	
11. C		23. C	
12. C		24. A	

Practice Test 7
Problem Solving

1. C		12. E	
2. D		13. A	
3. D		14. D	
4. E		15. C	
5. B		16. B	
6. E		17. A	
7. C		18. D	
8. C		19. E	
9. D		20. D	
10. C		21. E	
11. E		22. E	

Practice Test 8
Computation

1. C		14. E	
2. D		15. A	
3. E		16. C	
4. D		17. B	
5. E		18. A	
6. A		19. B	
7. A		20. B	
8. D		21. D	
9. B		22. B	
10. C		23. E	
11. E		24. D	
12. D		25. B	
13. C			

© Scholastic Inc.